YOUR KNOWLEDGE HAS VALUE

- We will publish your bachelor's and master's thesis, essays and papers

- Your own eBook and book - sold worldwide in all relevant shops

- Earn money with each sale

Upload your text at www.GRIN.com
and publish for free

Bibliographic information published by the German National Library:

The German National Library lists this publication in the National Bibliography; detailed bibliographic data are available on the Internet at http://dnb.dnb.de .

This book is copyright material and must not be copied, reproduced, transferred, distributed, leased, licensed or publicly performed or used in any way except as specifically permitted in writing by the publishers, as allowed under the terms and conditions under which it was purchased or as strictly permitted by applicable copyright law. Any unauthorized distribution or use of this text may be a direct infringement of the author s and publisher s rights and those responsible may be liable in law accordingly.

Imprint:

Copyright © 2017 GRIN Verlag, Open Publishing GmbH
Print and binding: Books on Demand GmbH, Norderstedt Germany
ISBN: 9783668463547

This book at GRIN:

http://www.grin.com/en/e-book/359321/secure-password-policy-current-situation-and-solutions

Shiva Reddy, Saikat Sinha, G. Abirami

Secure Password Policy. Current Situation and Solutions

GRIN Publishing

GRIN - Your knowledge has value

Since its foundation in 1998, GRIN has specialized in publishing academic texts by students, college teachers and other academics as e-book and printed book. The website www.grin.com is an ideal platform for presenting term papers, final papers, scientific essays, dissertations and specialist books.

Visit us on the internet:

http://www.grin.com/

http://www.facebook.com/grincom

http://www.twitter.com/grin_com

Secure Password Policy

A.Shiva Prasad Reddy
Department of CSE
SRM University

Saikat Sinha
Department of CSE
SRM University

Abirami.G
Assistant Professor, Dept. of CSE
SRM University

Abstract— Passwords are simple yet it is a critical component in most of the security systems. As it needs to protect the secure information of the user so it required being more secure and hard for the third party to crack on to a system. So it is important to provide a best password policy creation and management of policy is important so we need to provide a universal policy so that everyone can use it. In this paper we implemented, the most used password policy and difference of old policy and our policy. Finally, we show visualized data and implementation of the password policy in real time.

Contents

I. INTRODUCTION 2
  A. Collecting and testing 2
II. Measuring password strength 2
III. Results 3
IV. Multilingual password 4
V. location based tracking 4
VI. multiway authentication 4
VII. related 5
VIII. Conclusion 5
References 6

I. INTRODUCTION

Many things have changed in past few years and yet password policy remains and authentication process remains same which is by using username and password more over most of the password contains username with different combinations which can be guessed by a hacker and can be a victim of the hacker. As everyone dependent on the password to protect their personal and other information so it requires more secure mechanisms to protect data[4].

Textual passwords are most commonly used in most of the systems that include banking sector and social media etc. Which carry most extremely sensitive information of the user. Yet there is no universal password policy while every organization uses different password policy and makes harder for the user to remember the password by using symbols and numbers etc. Password datasets.

In our work, we collect a large number of leaked database of passwords to analyze.in our process, we come across with leaked passwords from LinkedIn and Reddit and most famous rock you database which helped us to analyze the trends in the recent passwords and helped us to make a more secure password policy.as we can see there has been more than 3-4 times passwords has been leaked from past five years .our work is even if passwords are leaked it would be hard for the hacker to enter into user account since the passwords are in different languages

A. Collecting and testing

Passwords are mostly easy to guess and many of us use most common words which include name or name followed by a number or by date of birth year which makes them easy to guess first, we collected data from different leaked databases[2] which include Myspace LinkedIn etc. Since the data is in the CSV format we used a tool called jupyter notebook to analyses the data and performed following operations includes[4]:

1. To find most commonly used passwords.[21]
2. Most common account name with actual username.
3. Hacked weather the username is equal to password.
4. Most commonly used passwords with user name.
5. Most used numbers in the passwords.
6. Checked character length in each password.
7. Minimum length passwords used.
8. Amount of time to crack the password by using brute force.[18]

II. MEASURING PASSWORD STRENGTH

Password strength is the measure of resistance to the guessing and by brute force attacks. It is the time required to crack the given password and it also include length and complexity and other aspects.

There are some steps for measuring password strength[15]:

1. Passwords less the 8 character are considered weak and easily crackable
2. If it contains complete alphabetic then it would be discouraged
3. It should contain a combination of symbols and numbers
4. The user should choose a password in such a way that it should not contain the name in the password
5. Instructions for the good password choosing should be provided
6. If it is auto-generated which would be more secure since it follows all rules etc.

III. RESULTS

Fig.1 The 50 Most used passwords visualized data[3]

Fig.2 visualized data Based on different characteristics

Fig.3 shows the visualized data of different words

Fig.4 shows the most used numbers at the end and least used passwords

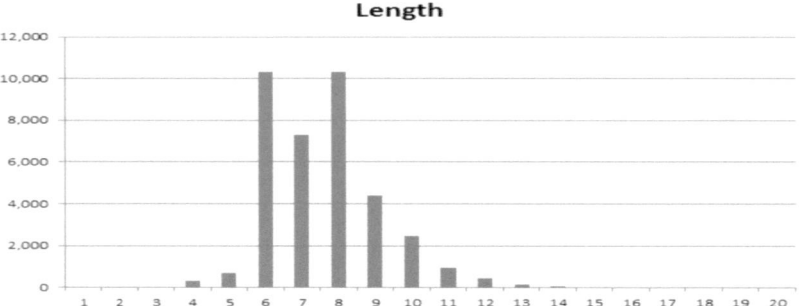

Fig.5 shows the relation between the length of character and number of users using it[22]

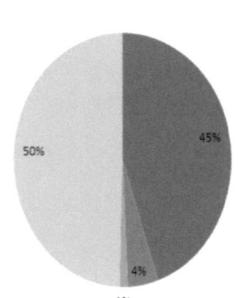

Fig.6 character type exclusivity example(lowerletters and numbers etc..)

IV. MULTILINGUAL PASSWORD

Most of the websites use English as their standard language to take input from the user, so it would be easy for the hacker to choose the language as English and apply brute force. If we provide multi-language support for the password policy it would take more time to crack the password and even if the passwords are leaked, hacker has to find the specific language to enter the password. So it would make the password hacking more complex.

V. LOCATION BASED TRACKING

The location based tracking will be used to safe guard users from getting hacked once their password is being compromised. The Location based tracking will utilise the location services of the device to keep a copy of the location where the user last logged in and it will also check the after a certain period of time the user logs back it will again access the user location if the user is out of range of that last logged in location and the time in between. Then the users, account will be assumed as compromised.

VI. MULTIWAY AUTHENTICATION

multi-way authentication can be other than password which would add multi-layer support which can be done by using OTP[9] (one time generated password or by using a random number generation method used by popular applications like steam etc. by this even if the user information is compromised attacker require an OTP to access the credential of the user

VII. RELATED

In the past few years, there are some modifications in password policy which include changing the password length from one character to six characters then later it has been changed to eight characters making it a standard length. But previously there were no restrictions on the number of alphabets and numbers and symbols and later there were a lot of changes and different organization uses different policy and there is no standard policy for everyone. And when it comes to encryption each organization use different encryption policy which is not disclosed to people. And there are a number of projects based on the visualization of password but none of them included the password analysis in different language input since most of the textual passwords are in English letters.

VIII. CONCLUSION

Traditional password strength metrics are becoming inefficient against the new generation of most advanced password guessing attacks that are being used against real applications. In this context, new and more reliable approaches for the estimation of password robustness are required to protect users against potential external threats as shown by the drastic change of direction with respect to previous versions of NIST's latest draft of recommendation SP 800-63-3. So by using Multilanguage support and location-based tracking we can provide a complex ready to go web application which can be implemented and secure than the usual password policy

References

1. Al-Ameen, M.N., Wright, M., Scielzo, S.: Towards making random passwords memorable: Leveraging users' cognitive ability through multiple cues. In: Proc. ACM CHI 2015. pp. 1–10. Seoul, Republic of Korea (April 18-23 2015)
2. Alexander, T.: Leaked passwords (July, 2012), http://thepasswordproject.com /leaked_password_lists_and_dictionaries
3. Allan, C.: 32 million Rockyou passwords stolen (Dec 2009), http://www.hardware heaven.com/news.php?newsid=526
4. Bauman, E., Lu, Y., Lin, Z.: Half a century of practice: Who is still storing plaintext passwords? In: Lopez, J., Wu, Y. (eds.) ISPEC 2015, LNCS, vol. 9065, pp. 253–267. Springer-Verlag (2015)
5. Bishop, M., V Klein, D.: Improving system security via proactive password checking. Computer & Security 14(3), 233–249 (1995)
6. Bonneau, J.: The science of guessing: Analyzing an anonymized corpus of 70 million passwords. In: IEEE S&P 2012. pp. 538–552. San Francisco, USA (May 21-23 2012)
7. Bonneau, J., Preibusch, S.: The password thicket: Technical and market failures in human authentication on the web. In: Proc. WEIS 2010 (June 7-8 2010)
8. Burnett, M.: 10,000 top passwords (June 2011), https://xato.net/passwords/m ore-top-worst-passwords/
9. Burr, W., Dodson, D., Perlner, R., Polk, W., Gupta, S., Nabbus, E.: NIST SP800- 63 – electronic authentication guideline. Tech. rep., NIST, Reston, VA (April 2006)
10. Carnavalet, X., Mannan, M.: From very weak to very strong: Analyzing passwordstrength meters. In: Proc. NDSS 2014. pp. 1–16. San Diego, CA, USA (2014)
11. Chiasson, S., van Oorschot, P.C.: Quantifying the security advantage of password expiration policies. Designs, Codes and Cryptography (2015), in press, Doi: http: //dx.doi.org/10.1007/s10623-015-0071-9
12. CNNIC: CNNIC Released the 35th Statistical Report on Internet Development in China (Feb 2015), http://www.apira.org/news.php?id=1732
13. Das, A., Bonneau, J., Caesar, M., Borisov, N., Wang, X.: The tangled web of password reuse. In: Proc. NDSS 2014. pp. 1–15 (2014)
14. DISA for DoD: Application security and development. Tech. rep., Defense Information Systems Agency (DISA), Reston, VA (July, 2013), doi: http://www.stigvi ewer.com/stig/application_security_and_development/
15. Egelman, S., Sotirakopoulos, A., Beznosov, K., Herley, C.: Does my password go up to eleven?: the impact of password meters on password selection. In: Proc. CHI 2013. pp. 2379–2388. ACM (2013)
16. Florencio, D., Herley, C.: A large-scale study of web password habits. In: Proc. WWW 2007. pp. 657–666. ACM (2007)
17. Flor˜encio, D., Herley, C.: Where do security policies come from? In: Proc. ACM SOUPS 2010. pp. 1–14. ACM, Redmond, Washington, USA (July 14-16 2010)
18. Furnell, S.: An assessment of website password practices. Computers & Security 26(7), 445–451 (2007)
19. Furnell, S.: Assessing password guidance and enforcement on leading websites. Computer Fraud & Security 2011(12), 10–18 (2011)
20. Furnell, S., B¨ar, N.: Essential lessons still not learned? Examining the password practices of end-users and service providers. In: Proc. HAS 2013, LNCS, vol. 8030, pp. 217–225. Springer (2013)
21. Goldman, J.: Chinese Hackers Publish 20 Million Hotel Reservations (Dec 2013), http://www.esecurityplanet.com/hackers/chinese-hackers-pub lish-20-million-hotel-reservations.html
22. Goodin, D.: Anatomy of a hack: How crackers ransack passwords like "qeadzcwrsfxv1331" (May, 2013), http://arstechnica.com/security/2013/05/how-c rackers-make-minced-meat-out-of-your-passwords/2/

YOUR KNOWLEDGE HAS VALUE

- We will publish your bachelor's and master's thesis, essays and papers

- Your own eBook and book - sold worldwide in all relevant shops

- Earn money with each sale

Upload your text at www.GRIN.com
and publish for free